Distinctions in Nature

Nocturnal and Diurnal Animals Explained

Alicia Z. Klepeis

Cavendish Square

New York

Published in 2017 by Cavendish Square Publishing, LLC
243 5th Avenue, Suite 136, New York, NY 10016

Copyright © 2017 by Cavendish Square Publishing, LLC

First Edition

CPSIA Compliance Information: Batch #CW17CSQ

All websites were available and accurate when this book was sent to press.

Library of Congress Cataloging-in-Publication Data

Names: Klepeis, Alicia, 1971- author.
Title: Nocturnal and diurnal animals explained / Alicia Z. Klepeis.
Description: New York : Cavendish Square Publishing, [2017] |
Series: Distinctions in nature | Includes bibliographical references and index.
Identifiers: LCCN 2016021851| ISBN 9781502621757 (library bound) |
ISBN 9781502621733 (pbk.) | ISBN 9781502621740 (6 pack) | ISBN 9781502621764 (ebook)
Subjects: LCSH: Nocturnal animals–Juvenile literature. |
Animal behavior–Juvenile literature. | Adaptation (Biology)–Juvenile literature.
Classification: LCC QL755.5 .K54 2017 | DDC 591.5/18–dc23

LC record available at https://lccn.loc.gov/2016021851

Editorial Director: David McNamara
Editor: Fletcher Doyle
Copy Editor: Nathan Heidelberger
Associate Art Director: Amy Greenan
Designer: Stephanie Flecha
Production Coordinator: Karol Szymczuk
Photo Research: J8 Media

The photographs in this book are used by permission and through the courtesy of:
Cover (Owl) Heinz Hudelist/imageBROKER/Getty Images; (Chimpanzee) Sis Kambou/AFP/Getty Images; p. 4 Khlongwangchao/Shutterstock; pp. 6, 16 Michael Durham/Minden Pictures/Getty Images; p. 7 Joel Sartore/National Geographic/Getty Images; p. 8 NajaShots/iStockphoto.com; p. 10 (Giraffe) Tier Und Naturfotografie J und C Sohns/Getty Images, (Leopard) Villiers Steyn/Shutterstock; p. 11 ESP Imaging/iStockphoto.com; p. 13 Steve Maslowski/Science Source/Getty Images; p. 14 Per-Gunnar Ostby/Oxford Scientific/Getty Images; p. 15 Zoran Kolundzija/iStockphoto.com; p. 17 Frans Lanting/Mint Images/Getty Images; p. 18 Tom Brakefield/Stockbyte/Getty Images; p. 19 PhotoBarmaley/Shutterstock.com; p. 20 (Wolf) Francesco Reginato/The Image Bank/Getty Images, (Hawk) Gregory Johnston/Shutterstock.com; p. 22 (Aardvark) Christian Colista/Shutterstock.com, (Turkey) Mark Herreid/Shutterstock.com; p. 24 Marcel Alsemgeest/Shutterstock.com; p. 26 (Rabbit) Roger de la Harpe/Gallo Images/Getty Images, (Elephants) John Michael Evan potter/Shutterstock.com, (Snake) Wayne Lynch/All Canada Photos/Getty Images.

Printed in the United States of America

Contents

A butterfly feeds on nectar from flowers during the daytime.

Introduction: Night and Day

I t's a sunny spring day. You walk to a nearby park. Squirrels scurry about with acorns in their mouths. Chickadees call to each other in the branches of trees. A butterfly lands on a flower. It sips **nectar** before moving on. All of these animals are **diurnal**. That means they are active during the day.

If you visited the same park late at night, you'd find different animals there. Moths might be flitting near the park's lampposts. An owl could be hooting from a tree. Raccoons might be grabbing food from trashcans, using their

A barn owl flaps its wings while hunting in the darkness of night.

well-designed paws. Animals that are active at night are called **nocturnal**.

Diurnal and nocturnal animals have some things in common. They live all over the world. They make homes for themselves. They mate and raise babies. But

Opossum mothers sometimes carry their babies when looking for food.

these animals can also be different from each other. Nocturnal animals have excellent night vision. Diurnal critters have better color vision and see in more detail. Nocturnal animals have a better sense of hearing than diurnal animals.

Scientists **classify** animals, or put them into different groups, based on their features. **Taxonomy** is the process of classifying **organisms**.

A box turtle wanders in the grass during the daytime.

1 Viewing Nocturnal and Diurnal Animals

Some animals are active during the daytime. Have you ever seen a turtle shuffling through the grass in the sunshine? Then you have seen a diurnal animal. The word "diurnal" comes from the Latin word meaning "daily." People are diurnal.

Diurnal Animals

There are many diurnal animals in the world. You might see squirrels and butterflies in your

By day, a giraffe eats leaves that are high in the trees.

A leopard sleeps in a tree during the day.

backyard. What if you went to Africa? Gorillas and giraffes eat, play, and find mates during the day.

Nocturnal Animals

Nocturnal animals are active at night. Moths and raccoons are examples. So are many big cats, such as lions and lynx. Nocturnal animals sleep the days away. They often hide while snoozing. This keeps them out of sight of **predators**.

Zoom In

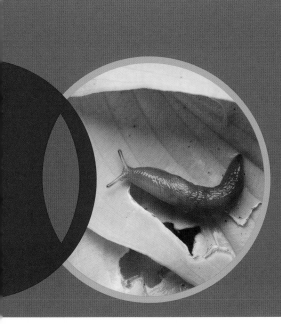

Slugs are nocturnal animals. Their bodies would dry up if they spent their days in the sunshine. That would kill them.

Why are some animals active at night? Some animals, like opossums, feel safer at night than during the day. Other nocturnal animals have colors that are better hidden at night. By hunting after dark, night creatures don't have to compete for food with diurnal animals. This lets more animals live in the same **habitat**.

Nocturnal animals have been around since the days of the dinosaurs. Far more animals are active at night than during the day.

A group of raccoons have a nighttime feast from an open garbage can.

2 8 Comparing Nocturnal and Diurnal Animals

I n addition to the times when they are active, diurnal and nocturnal animals are different in other ways. Most of the distinctions are in the way they use their senses.

Vision

Some nocturnal animals have very big eyes with large **pupils**. These eyes let in lots of light. However, they can't see colors. An owl's eyes are so big that they cannot move inside its head! Instead, the owl must turn its head to see in different directions. Some

A cat's eyes glow in the dark, thanks to the tapetum.

night animals have eyes that appear to glow in the dark. This is due to a layer in their eyes called the **tapetum**. This layer reflects light back into the eye, allowing it to be seen twice.

Diurnal animals can see colors. They also see a sharper image than nocturnal animals. Humans can see three colors. These colors combine to form the many colors we see every day. Birds can see more colors, and they can see **ultraviolet** (UV) light. They use colors to mate and find food. Some small animals give off UV light, allowing birds of prey to see them from high in the sky.

Many nocturnal animals have split pupils that close more tightly than the round pupils that people have. This protects their light-sensitive eyes.

Hearing and Echolocation

Nocturnal animals often have great hearing. Many night creatures have bigger ears than diurnal animals.

A fennec fox listens for prey in the desert. Its ears radiate heat.

A bat swoops down to catch an insect in mid-flight, using echolocation.

Fennec foxes are the smallest foxes on Earth, but they have the largest ears. These night hunters can hear lizards, mice, and insects from far away. The ears of barn owls are at different heights on the animal's head. This helps them hear if a sound is coming from above or below.

Bats can't see well. They make high squeaking noises as they fly. If these squeaks hit an insect, the sound bounces back off of it. The bat hears the bounced-off squeak (echo). It swoops in on its **prey**. This system of bouncing sounds off objects is called **echolocation**.

Smell and Touch

Most birds don't have great senses of smell. However, nocturnal birds are often an exception to this rule. The kiwi bird of New Zealand looks for food in the dark. It has a super sniffer at the end of its beak. It can smell food below the soil.

Raccoons have an amazing sense of touch. They use their paws to feel their way up the branches of trees.

A kiwi forages at night. It can sniff tasty morsels under the forest floor..

Their front paws have five fingers. Raccoons use these fingers to grab nuts, berries, and even fish. They can also pry open trashcans!

Communication

All animals communicate. Many nocturnal animals use scent to communicate. Skunks release a stinky spray

The black-and-white pattern of a skunk may warn predators to beware.

Nocturnal and Diurnal Animals Explained

Zoom In

The tarsier has the biggest eyes, relative to its body size, of any mammal in the world. Each of the tarsier's eyeballs is as big as its entire brain!

from **glands** under their tails. This warns others to stay away!

Fireflies use light to communicate in the darkness. They are able to make light by mixing **chemicals** inside of their bodies. Male fireflies flash their lights on and off. Females are attracted to flash patterns.

1. A wolf howls by moonlight. Wolves are the largest members of the dog family.

2. A red-tailed hawk soars in daylight, seeking prey in the fields below.

3 Be an Animal Detective

Review the characteristics of each of the animals in the questions below, and decide if they are nocturnal or diurnal. Then tell us why.

1. Wolves call to each other when it's dark outside. They howl to keep outsiders away and to communicate with other members of their pack.

2. The red-tailed hawk has excellent vision. It can see colors in the ultraviolet range. The red-tailed hawk spies and hunts prey as it flies overhead during the daytime.

3. By night, an aardvark sniffs around for its next meal.

4. A turkey seeks berries, nuts, snails, and insects during the day.

Nocturnal and Diurnal Animals Explained

3. An aardvark has a long snout and long ears. Its sense of smell and its hearing are excellent. It can sniff out ants and termites even in the dark. It uses its long, sticky tongue to collect around fifty thousand insects in a night.

4. Wild turkeys travel in flocks. By day, they gather berries, nuts, and insects to eat. At night, turkeys fly into trees and **roost**.

A couple of deer are on the move at twilight.

4 Rule Breakers

Not every animal falls neatly into the categories of diurnal or nocturnal. Some are rule breakers.

Rabbits and deer are not diurnal or nocturnal. They are **crepuscular**, or most active at dawn and dusk. This schedule helps rabbits avoid predators that hunt during the day or at night as much as possible. Also, crepuscular animals avoid the heat of the day and the cold at night.

A rabbit nibbles grass as the sun goes down.

Elephants and Snakes

Some animals are active both during the day and the night. Elephants are one such creature. These big beasts like to rest during the heat of the day. But they range about and eat both by sunlight and moonlight.

Some snakes can be also both diurnal and nocturnal, depending on the season. For example, the gopher

An elephant herd travels by day. These huge animals also move around at night.

A gopher snake suns itself during the day. It stays active in all but the hottest weather.

snake and the copperhead are diurnal most of the year. But when the daytime heat gets to be too much, they become nocturnal.

The next time you're outside, check out the animals. Can you tell which are diurnal and which are nocturnal?

chemical A compound or substance that has been prepared or purified.

classify To arrange in or assign to categories based on shared characteristics.

crepuscular Active mainly around sunrise and sundown.

diurnal Active mainly in the daytime.

echolocation A process for finding distant or invisible objects by using high-pitched sound waves reflected back to the sender from the object.

gland An organ in a human or animal body that makes particular chemical substances either for discharge into the surroundings or use in the body.

habitat The place or kind of place where an animal or plant naturally lives or grows.

nectar A sweet liquid given off by plants, particularly by the flowers.

nocturnal Active mainly at night.

organism An individual plant, animal, or single-celled life form.

predator An animal that survives by killing and eating other animals.

prey An animal that is hunted or killed for food by another animal.

pupil The opening in the iris of the eye that contracts and expands to control how much light enters the eye.

roost To settle down for sleep or rest.

tapetum A reflective layer in the eyes of many animals, causing them to shine in the dark.

taxonomy The orderly classification of plants and animals according to their natural relationships.

ultraviolet Located beyond the visible (to humans) spectrum at its violet end and having a wavelength longer than X-rays.

Books

De La Bédoyère, Camilla. *Creatures of the Night.* Buffalo, NY: Firefly Books Inc., 2014.

Niver, Heather Moore. *Badgers After Dark.* Animals of the Night. New York: Enslow Publishing, 2016.

Rabe, Tish. *Out of Sight Till Tonight!: All About Nocturnal Animals.* New York: Random House, 2015.

Websites

Arizona-Sonora Desert Museum
http://www.desertmuseum.org/kids/oz/long-fact-sheets/Title%20Page.php
Learn about the animals of the Sonoran Desert.

National Wildlife Federation
http://www.nwf.org/news-and-magazines/national-wildlife/birds/archives/2012/bird-vision.aspx
This article describes the way birds see.

Index

Page numbers in **boldface** are illustrations.

About the Author

Alicia Z. Klepeis loves to research fun and out-of-the-ordinary topics that make nonfiction exciting for readers. Alicia began her career at the National Geographic Society. She is the author of many kids' books, including *The World's Strangest Foods*, *Bizarre Things We've Called Medicine*, *Francisco's Kites*, and *From Pizza to Pisa*. She lives with her family in upstate New York.